W9-AVB-752

NORTH HAMPTON PUBLIC LIBRARY
237A Atlantic Avenue
North Hampton, NH 03862
603-964-6326
www.nhplib.org

Hummer

Tracy Nelson Maurer

NORTH HAMPTON PUBLIC LIBRARY
237A Atlantic Avenue
North Hampton, NH 03862
603-964-6326
www.nhplib.org

Rourke
Publishing LLC
Vero Beach, Florida 32964

J629.222

© 2007 Rourke Publishing LLC

All rights reserved. No part of this book may be reproduced or utilized in any form or by any means, electronic or mechanical including photocopying, recording, or by any information storage and retrieval system without permission in writing from the publisher.

www.rourkepublishing.com

We recognize that some words, model names and designations, for example, mentioned herein are the property of the trademark holder. We use them for identification purposes only. This is not an official publication.

PHOTO CREDITS: Courtesy of Hummer X Club: pages 13, 16, 21, 24, 26-27, 28, 28-29; Courtesy of the Department of Defense: pages 4, 5, 10 (bottom), 6-7, 6 (bottom), 7 (bottom), 8, 8-9, 9 (bottom), 29 (bottom); Courtesy of American General: pages 12, 15; © Armentrout: pages 10-11, 14, 18-19, 20, 22-23, 23, 24-25

AUTHOR CREDITS:
The author gratefully acknowledges project assistance provided by Jeffrey Vang and Kelly Hines at Wally McCarthy's Cadillac-Hummer, Roseville, Minnesota.

Also, the author extends appreciation to Mike Maurer, Lois M. Nelson, Margaret and Thomas, and the team at Rourke.

Editor: Robert Stengard-Olliges

Cover Design: Todd Field
Page Design: Nicola Stratford

Library of Congress Cataloging-in-Publication Data

Maurer, Tracy, 1965-
  Hummer / Tracy Nelson Maurer.
    p. cm. -- (Full throttle)
  Includes bibliographical references and index.
  ISBN 1-60044-222-6 (hardcover)
  ISBN 978-1-60044-362-6 (paperback)
 1. Hummer H2 sport utility vehicle--Juvenile literature. 2. Hummer H3 sport utility vehicle--Juvenile literature. 3. Hummer trucks--Juvenile literature. 4. Hummer H1 truck--Juvenile literature. I. Title. II. Series: Maurer, Tracy, 1965-. Full throttle.
  TL235.65.H86M 38 2006
  629.222'2--dc22

                    2006017521

Printed in the USA

CG/CG

Rourke Publishing

www.rourkepublishing.com – sales@rourkepublishing.com
Post Office Box 3328, Vero Beach, FL 32964

Table of Contents

The Military's Mighty 4x4

Hummers and Jeeps, two **4x4** legends, trace their roots to the Willys-Overland Company. Willys-Overland built 4x4 jeeps for the U.S. Army in the 1940s. Jeeps worked so well that the military used them through World War II, the Korean Conflict, the Vietnam War, and in peaceful times until the 1980s.

Along the way, the Willys-Overland Company changed owners several times. Today's Jeeps are built mainly for **civilians**. (That's a story for a different book.)

The military jeep gave way to the High Mobility Multipurpose Wheeled Vehicle (HMMWV), or Humvee, made by AM General Corporation. AM General also builds civilian Hummers for General Motors Corporation to sell.

Build a Better Jeep

Military jeeps were no slackers. When the U.S. Army asked for an updated type of jeep in 1979, military vehicle manufacturers knew it was a steep task. What could possibly replace a jeep?

- A simple-to-maintain machine based on advanced technology
- A sturdy, safe vehicle that wouldn't roll over easily
- A strong transporter able to carry 1.25 tons (1.13 metric tons) of cargo
- A flexible platform that could adapt to handle many different jobs
- A lightweight model that could pack into airplanes for distant missions
- A rugged all-terrain king that could climb a 22-inch (56-cm) vertical wall, tackle a 60-percent grade, wade through 30 inches (76 cm) of water, and command 16 inches (46 cm) of ground clearance... All of that rolled into one amazing package.

4x4
  a vehicle that moves by a system that can send power to all four wheels
civilians
  people who are not soldiers or police

The Army staged more than 400 wicked tests for prototypes from three different companies. The long, squat, and ready-to-rip 4x4 Humvee from AM General proved itself worthy to replace the jeep.

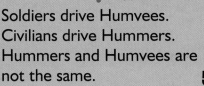

Soldiers drive Humvees. Civilians drive Hummers. Hummers and Humvees are not the same.

One Platform Goes a Long Way

For the first delivery, AM General built five Humvee models and adapted them to make 15 different vehicles. These versions included troop carriers, pick-up trucks, ambulances, machine-gun carriers, mobile grenade launchers, and mobile anti-aircraft and anti-tank missile launchers. According to AM General, the Humvee has sported more than 65 combat and combat-support systems since 1985.

*Humvee models share the same diesel engine design, **chassis**, and **transmission** system. The single platform saves training time for drivers and mechanics. It also saves money in making parts.*

All Humvees share more than 40 of the same parts.

chassis
> the frame that supports the body of a vehicle

transmission
> in vehicles, the unit of gears that transfers the engine's power to move the wheels

Water doesn't stop a Humvee. It can plow through depths of 2.5 feet (0.8 meter). Some Humvees have special equipment, such as an engine snorkel, to handle five feet (1.5 meters) of water.

Fäst Fäct

A dashboard switch starts the Humvee engine. No lost keys on the battlefield!

Changing for New Missions

The Humvee continues to change and improve. Some upgrades add power, such as the 6.5-liter V-8 diesel engine. Other features allow the Humvee to carry new communication tools or weapons. New missions and new dangers challenge Humvee designers to create stronger, faster, safer, and simply better machines.

Fast Fact

Humvees use blackout light covers to aim the headlights down to the ground. Drivers can see the road but enemies can't see them coming.

M998 Truck Humvee

The squat Humvee is long and wide to avoid rollovers. With a sturdy steel chassis and a lightweight aluminum body, a Humvee M998 Truck starts at about 7,700 pounds (3,493 kg).

Length: 15 feet (4.5 meters)
Height: 5.75 feet (1.75 meters)
Width: 7 feet (2.13 meters)

*Roadside bombs and other dangers created a need for extra **ballistic** protection on Humvees. Some "up-armored" Humvees use steel plating on doors and under the cab plus bullet-barrier glass windows.*

ballistic
related to bullets or bombs

Fast Fact

Run-flat tires on Humvees allow soldiers to travel for 30 miles (48.25 km) on flat tires. They don't carry a spare tire.

Most Humvees top out at about 70 miles (112.65 km) per hour. The military is testing the Hybrid-Electric Humvee that uses fuel and a battery pack for power. It runs about 15 miles (24 km) per hour faster and a lot quieter than a standard Humvee.

The First: H1

Soldiers tested Humvees in real battle situations in 1989 when President George Bush sent troops to Panama. During Operation Desert Shield in 1991, television images of the powerful Humvees boosted interest in the vehicle back home.

AM General knew that Jeeps jumped from military use to civilian sales after World War II. Why not sell a street-legal version of the Humvee? In 1992, AM General started selling the first Hummers (later called H1s).

Fast Fact

Humvees should run for about 15 years. On missions in Iraq, the vehicles last about two years.

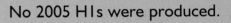

No 2005 H1s were produced.

AM General built the four-seater Hummer from 1992 until 2004. In 1999, the H1 name was added. The 2006 model featured so many upgrades that the company renamed it again, calling it H1 Alpha.

MILESTONES

1985 First Humvees rolled out of the AM General factory

1992 Civilians bought the first Hummers

1999 AM General and General Motors sealed their deal

2000 Hummer H2 concept vehicle wowed the Detroit Auto Show

2002 All-new H2s produced at the all-new Hummer factory

2005 Updated 2006 H1 Alpha reached dealerships

2005 First 2006 H3s available for sale

2006 General Motors announced the end of H1 Alpha production

"Model year" is usually one year ahead of when the vehicle is actually launched. So, the 2006 H3 reached dealerships in spring 2005.

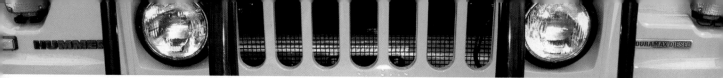

So Alike

The H1 Alpha is boldly similar to the military version. It even starts with the Humvee on the same factory production line. The H1 Alpha shares the boxy design and impressive ground clearance. It climbs 60-percent grades and handles 40-degree side slopes—just like the warrior wagon. It slips through 30-inches (76 cm) of water like the Humvee, too (but the H1 Alpha's electrical system is not watertight).

Some Details H1 Alpha and Hummer Share

- Aircraft-quality, rust-resistant, and riveted aluminum body
- Vertical windshield that doesn't reflect light up to enemy aircraft
- Heavy-duty, box steel frame
- Rugged off-road suspension system
- Small steering wheel to fit driver with a bulky ammunition belt
- High-riding drivetrain mechanicals housed in the center floor bulge
- Drains in the cabin floor

U.S. parts make up nearly 100 percent of Hummers, among the highest of any American vehicle.

four-wheel drive
a system that transfers the engine's power to all four wheels

Humvees and Hummers use independent, full-time **four-wheel drive**. *The system makes sure that any wheel with traction keeps moving. Even if three wheels lose their grip, at least one still crawls along.*

The H1 Alpha's 9000-pound (4082 kg) weight makes it a heavy-duty Class III truck—not a Sport Utility Vehicle (SUV). Because of its height, the H1 Alpha must have lights along its roof.

AM General offers a Central Tire Inflation System (CTIS) on Humvees and the H1 Alpha. A dashboard control adjusts air in each tire even while the vehicle is moving.

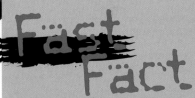

Releasing air in tires gains traction in sandy or soft terrain. Adding air protects tires at faster speeds on smooth highways.

So Different

HI Alpha Has Luxuries That Humvee Doesn't:

- Top-end sound system
- Leather seats and carpeting
- Windows and power window controls
- Power door locks
- Cupholders
- Key start
- Dome light
- Rich paint in a range of colors

turbocharger
a special fan turned by the engine's exhaust gases that works to pump more air into the cylinders and boost power output

torque
a measure of mechanical strength or turning force

A beastly 6.6-liter, diesel V-8 engine with a **turbocharger** rumbles under the HI Alpha hood. It's the only diesel Hummer. It delivers 520 lbs.-ft. **torque** and 300 horsepower—that's 46 percent more horsepower than before.

Fast Fact

Even with all its bulk, the off-road king rips from 0 to 60 miles (97 km) per hour in just 13.5 seconds.

The Generals Agree

Early on, the explosive interest in Hummers—and ideas for an all-new H2—prompted AM General to think about linking its high-quality production experience with another company. The proven **marketing** knowledge of General Motors made a good fit.

The two Generals sealed a unique deal in December 1999: AM General would manufacture Hummers and military Humvees, while General Motors would own the Hummer brand name and sell the civilian models.

The two companies also agreed to develop a new Hummer, called the H2—*and* build a completely *new* factory to produce it. *Then get this:* they announced they would do all that in just two years! Most carmakers take three years to update an existing model made in an existing plant.

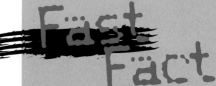

marketing
activities to help move products from manufacturer to buyer, including advertising, shipping, and selling

Before the deal with AM General, General Motors had started on ideas for a super SUV, code-named "The Chunk."

Sharing Ideas

To speed the new Hummer H2 development, GM shared its plans for the GMT-800 chassis. The H2 designers borrowed only what met Hummer performance standards.

On Time

AM General and General Motors kept their promise and revealed the H2 production model at the Los Angeles Auto Show in 2002.

The GMT-800 chassis later appeared on Chevrolet and GMC full-size trucks and SUVs, such as the Tahoe, Yukon, Suburban, and Escalade.

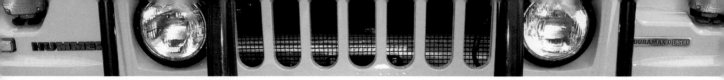

Ready as Promised

Like they said they would, AM General and GM built a new 630,000-square-foot (60,387-sq. m) factory to produce the H2 in about 14 months. Today, the Mishawaka, Indiana plant can finish about 46,000 H2s yearly. Next door, a 570,000-square-foot (52,955-sq. m) plant builds Humvees.

Inside the H2 factory, each vehicle takes a dip into a huge tank for an even base coat. Robots precisely spray about five gallons of paint and clearcoat to each H2.

True to Hummer standards, the H2 was designed for off-road performance first. Everything else came second. What can the H2 do?

- Climb a 60% grade
- Handle a 40% side slope
- Conquer a 16-inch (46 cm) vertical wall
- Ford up to 20 inches (51 cm) of water

Instead of standard coil springs, the H2 offers off-roading air suspension. It can raise the rear by two inches to lift over obstacles.

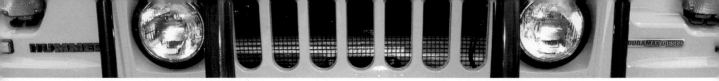

Today's H2 stands a few inches taller and longer than the H1 Alpha to fit six passengers instead of four. The H2's massive wheels and tires reach three feet (one meter) high. Even a long-legged driver stretches on the 24-inch (61 cm) step into the rig.

The H2's 6.0-liter V-8 pumps out 325 horsepower and 365 lbs.-ft. torque. It can nail 0 to 60 miles (97 km) per hour in just 9.9 seconds. Not bad for a 6,400-pound (2,903 kg) rig.

H2 SUT

Hummer introduced the H2 SUT (Sport Utility Truck) for sale in the summer of 2004. Its pick-up cargo area could be made longer by folding down the rear cabin window.

hydrogen
> a colorless, odorless, and burnable gas

Fuel Alternative

The Hummer might someday use **hydrogen** fuel. The H2H SUT concept with its modified V-8 engine uses far less gasoline than other motors. So far, the H2H can go about 60 miles (97 km) between hydrogen fill-ups.

Fast Fact

The Chevrolet Corvette Z06 motor inspired the H2 engine.

Baby Hummer

The 2006 H3 introduced the baby of the Hummer family. It's shorter than H2 by almost 17 inches (43 cm). Its price starts at under $30,000. The Hummer H3 borrowed a few platform ideas from the Chevrolet Colorado and GMC Canyon pick-ups. But it's still a Hummer, ready for road trips or trips without roads:

- Up to 39.4° approach and 36.5° departure angles
- Up to 9.1-inch (23.11 cm) ground clearance
- Approximate 37-foot (11.28 m) turning circle

With full-time 4x4 grip, the H3 fords 16 inches (46 cm) of water and climbs walls that high, too. And it's full of nonstop Hummer attitude.

The H3 weighs about 4,700 pounds (2132 kg).

H3 Packages

Buyers choose from two H3 packages. The H3 Adventure Series comes with a locking rear differential, full underbody protection, and other off-road features. The LUX Series (for "luxury") offers a decent off-road

Hummer H3X

In dealerships in late 2006, the 2007 Hummer H3X added a tricked-out look to the Luxury package. Think chrome, and loads of it—on the tube steps, fuel door, and brush guard.

machine spiffed up with heated leather seats, a serious sound system, and other cushy extras.

Both H3 packages sport a powerful 3.5-liter, inline 5-cylinder engine with an automatic or a manual transmission (the first manual for any Hummer). The H3 squeezes out 20 miles (8.5 km) per gallon. Although critics have blasted Hummers for poor fuel economy, the Hummers actually fare about as well as other big 4x4s.

23

Family Traits

The Humvee and H1 set the family look for Hummer. The boxy shape and small windows create the visual oomph. All Hummers have a seven-slot grille and round headlights to note the military heritage. The name "H-U-M-M-E-R" marches across the grille bars—as if somebody wouldn't know what it was.

The bare gas cap is part of the Hummer style.

Hummer door handles, grille bars, and many other "chrome" items are actually really tough plastic.

Side clips hold the hood on all Hummers. On the H1 and H2, the hood hinges open at the grille. On the H3, the hood hinges open at the windshield.

Hummer Logo

The Hummer logo on the underbody armor announces which 4x4 is king of the hill. On most Hummers, strong metal skid plates protect the gas tank and other underbody parts that power the vehicle.

More Than Tough Enough

Hummers are more than tough enough for the toughest off-road adventures. How tough? Many owners try to find out over and over again! They test their Hummers in competitions and just-for-fun trail rides. Hummers have proven especially strong challengers at rock-crawling competitions and desert races.

Rod Hall

Legendary off-road driver Rod Hall joined Team Hummer in 1993. He and his son Chad have raced in the Baja 1000 and other desert races, sometimes winning by hours.

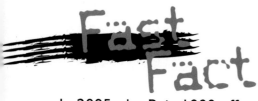

In 2005, the Baja 1000 off-road course looped from the city of Ensenada into the grueling Mexican desert and back. It covered more than 700 miles (1,126.5 km).

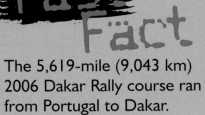

Fäst
Fäct

The 5,619-mile (9,043 km) 2006 Dakar Rally course ran from Portugal to Dakar. Since the 1970s, the two-week race has changed routes every year.

Robby Gordon

Champion driver Robby Gordon tested the Hummer H3 in the off-road 2006 Dakar Rally. The H3 held leading positions until a crash halted the attempt. Watch for the H3 at the finish line in coming years.

Race fans tell this story:

Back in the U.S. just after testing the H3 in the 2006 Dakar Rally, Robby Gordon washed the truck and filled the gas tank. That's about all he could do: the truck's spare parts hadn't arrived from Dakar yet. Then he drove the H3 directly to the Best in the Desert Parker "425" race in Arizona and won the Trophy Truck division.

More amazing, Robby drove the street-legal H3 race truck home afterward.

Today, many Hummer owners compete in just-for-fun events and simply enjoy driving their super-tough 4x4s to off-road places to fish, camp, and relax. Some owners belong to The Hummer Club, and join its driving trips and group outings. They explore local trails, private facilities, and 4x4 paradises such as Moab, Utah. Hummer dealerships also sponsor events and competitions.

*Each Hummer dealership usually includes a small off-road demonstration course. Dealers also sell **aftermarket** parts, such as brush grille guards, off-road spotlights, and steps.*

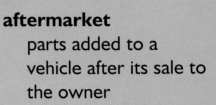

aftermarket
parts added to a vehicle after its sale to the owner

Fast Fact

Fifteen miles of obstacle-pitted trails wind through mud bogs, climb rocky slopes, and sneak along treacherous wooded trails at the AM General test course.

Hummer owners often volunteer to help in rescue efforts and other charity work. HOPE (Hummer Owners Prepared for Emergencies) delivers relief to disaster victims by tapping the Hummers' ability to travel where other vehicles can't. From Humvees to Hummers, these full-throttle 4x4s continue to protect, serve, and roll out the fun!

29

Glossary

4x4 (FOR bih for) – a vehicle that moves by a system that can send power to all four wheels

aftermarket (AFF tur MAR kit) – parts added to a vehicle after its sale to the owner

ballistic (bah LISS tik) – related to bullets or bombs

chassis (CHASS ee) – the frame that supports the body of a vehicle

civilians (si VILL yenz) – people who are not soldiers or police

four-wheel drive (FOR WEEL drihv) – a system that transfers the engine's power to all four wheels

hydrogen (HI drah jen) – a colorless, odorless, and burnable gas

marketing (MAR ki ting) – activities to help move products from manufacturer to buyer, including advertising, shipping, and selling

torque (TORK) – a measure of mechanical strength or force produced by an engine

transmission (trans MISH un) – in vehicles, the unit of gears that transfers the engine's power to move the wheels

turbocharger (TUR boh char jur) – a special fan turned by the engine's exhaust gases that works to pump more air into the cylinders and boost power output

Further Reading

Edsall, Larry. *Hummer H3*. Motorbooks International, 2005.

Green, Michael. *Humvee at War*. Zenith Press, 2005.

Healy, Nick. *High Mobility Vehicles: The Humvees*. Capstone Press, 2005.

Maurer, Tracy Nelson. *Desert Racers*. Rourke Publishing, 2004.

Websites

www.amgeneral.com

auto.howstuffworks.com/four-wheel-drive9.htm

www.hummer.com

www.off-road.com

www.treadlightly.org

Index

About the Author

Tracy Nelson Maurer writes nonfiction and fiction books for children, including more than 50 titles for Rourke Publishing LLC. Tracy lives with her husband Mike and two children near Minneapolis, Minnesota.

NORTH HAMPTON PUBLIC LIBRARY
237A Atlantic Avenue
North Hampton, NH 03862
603-964-6326
www.nhplib.org